Retiring to Spain
Everything you need to know.

Arthur Crandon LL.B.(Hons), M.A.

Retiring to Spain. Everything you need to know
Copyright Arthur Crandon 2024

All rights reserved. No part of this book may be reproduced, stored in a retrieval system, or transmitted in any form or by any means—electronic, mechanical, photocopying, recording, or otherwise—without the prior written permission of the publisher, except for brief quotations in critical reviews or articles.

This is a work of fiction. Names, characters, places, and incidents are either the product of the author's imagination or used fictitiously. Any resemblance to actual persons, living or dead, events, or locales is entirely coincidental.

ISBN: 9798336313659

Cover design by Lynnie Ceniza

Interior design and formatting by Lynnie Ceniza

Published by Arthur Crandon Publishing

Visit our website: Arthurcrandon.co.uk

DISCLAIMER

The information provided in this book is for general informational purposes only. It does not constitute legal, financial, or professional advice. While every effort has been made to ensure accuracy, the author and publisher assume no responsibility for errors or omissions. Readers should consult with appropriate professionals for specific advice tailored to their individual circumstances.

First Edition: July 2024

Visit Arthurcrandon.co.uk for More titles.

VISIT ARTHURCRANDON.CO.UK

FOR MORE TITLES

Retirement to the Philippines made easy

K1 fiance visa to the us – fast track

Secrets to buying condos in the Philippines

Buying land in the Philippines

Annulment in the Philippines

Breaking free from a bad marriage

Get a visit visa to America the first time

Marriage in the Philippines

Get a visit visa to the United Kingdom

1	Visas and Residency	1
2	Healthcare	13
3	Financial Considerations	19
4	Housing	25
5	Cultural and Social	31
6	Taxation	37
7	Legal and Admin	43
8	Practical Steps	49

1 VISAS AND RESIDENCY

Non lucrative visa

Here's a detailed breakdown of the non-lucrative visa application process for British citizens retiring to Spain:

Eligibility

- **No work or professional activity**: you must not engage in any employment or professional activity in Spain. This visa is designed for those who can support themselves financially without working.

Financial requirements

- **Sufficient financial means**: as of 2024, you need to demonstrate an annual income of approximately €28,800 (400% of the iprem) for a single applicant. For each additional family member, you need an extra €7,200 per year (100% of the iprem).

- **Proof of funds**: acceptable sources of income include pensions, rental income, dividends, and other passive income. You will need to provide bank statements or other financial documents to prove you have sufficient funds.

Health insurance

- **Private health insurance**: you must have private health insurance that provides coverage equivalent to the Spanish public healthcare system. The insurance must be valid for at least one year and cover all medical expenses without co-payments.

Application process

1. **Gather required documents**:

    o **Passport**: valid for at least one year beyond the date of application.

- **Visa application form**: completed and signed.

- **Passport-sized photos**: recent photographs meeting the consulate's specifications.

- **Proof of financial means**: bank statements, pension statements, or other documents showing sufficient funds.

- **Health insurance**: proof of private health insurance coverage.

- **Criminal record certificate**: a certificate from the UK and any other country where you have lived in the past five years, showing no criminal record. This must be translated into Spanish and apostilled.

- **medical certificate**: a certificate from a doctor stating that you do not have any diseases that could pose a public health risk, translated into Spanish and apostilled.

2. **Submit your application**:

    o **Where to apply**: submit your application at the Spanish consulate in the UK. There are consulates in London, Manchester, and Edinburgh.

    o **Appointment**: schedule an appointment online through the consulate's website. Ensure you bring all required documents to your appointment.

3. **Application fee**:

    o Pay the visa application fee, which varies by consulate. Check the specific consulate's website for the current fee.

4. **Processing time**:

    o The processing time for the non-lucrative visa can take up to three months. It's advisable to apply well in advance of your planned move.

After arrival in spain

1. **Register with local authorities**:

    o **Empadronamiento**: register at your local town hall to get your certificate of registration (Empadronamiento).

    o **foreigner's identity number (nie)**: apply for your nie, which is necessary for various administrative processes in Spain.

2. **Residency card (tie)**:

    o Within one month of arrival, apply for your tarjeta de identidad de extranjero (tie) at the local immigration office. This card serves as your residency permit.

Renewal

- **First renewal**: the initial visa is valid for one year. You can renew it for two more years, provided you continue to meet the financial and residency requirements (spending at least 183 days per year in Spain).

- **Subsequent renewals**: after the first renewal, you can renew the visa for another two years. After five years of continuous residency, you may apply for long-term residency.

By following these steps and ensuring you meet all requirements, you can enjoy a smooth transition to your new life in Spain.

The Golden Visa

Here's a detailed breakdown of the Golden Visa for British citizens retiring to Spain:

Eligibility

- **Investment Requirement**: You must invest at least €500,000 in Spanish real estate. This investment must be made from your own funds, without using a mortgage for the initial €500,000.

- **Other Investment Options**: Alternatively, you can invest €1 million in Spanish bank deposits or shares of Spanish companies, or €2 million in Spanish public debt.

- **Age and Legal Requirements**: You must be over 18 years old, have no criminal record, and have private health insurance in Spain.

Benefits

- **Residency**: The Golden Visa grants you and your family the right to live in Spain. Initially, it is valid for one year, and can be renewed for two-year periods.

- **Work Authorization**: Unlike the Non-Lucrative Visa, the Golden Visa allows you to work in Spain.

- **Schengen Zone Travel**: You can travel freely within the Schengen Zone for up to 90 days in any 180-day period.

- **Family Inclusion**: Your spouse and dependent children can also obtain residency under your Golden Visa.

Application Process

1. **Gather Required Documents**:

    - **Passport**: Valid for at least one year beyond the date of application.

    - **Visa Application Form**: Completed and signed.

    - **Passport-Sized Photos**: Recent photographs meeting the consulate's specifications.

    - **Proof of Investment**: Documentation showing the purchase of real estate or other qualifying investments.

    - **Health Insurance**: Proof of private health insurance coverage.

    - **Criminal Record Certificate**: A certificate from the UK and any other country where you have lived in the past five years, showing no criminal record. This must be translated into Spanish and apostilled.

- **Proof of Funds**: Bank statements or other financial documents to demonstrate sufficient funds for the investment.

2. **Submit Your Application**:

    - **Where to Apply**: Submit your application at the Spanish consulate in the UK. There are consulates in London, Manchester, and Edinburgh.

    - **Appointment**: Schedule an appointment online through the consulate's website. Ensure you bring all required documents to your appointment.

3. **Application Fee**:

    - The fee for a single applicant is typically between €2,500 and €3,500. Renewal fees are similar.

4. **Processing Time**:

    - The processing time for the Golden Visa can be as short as 20 days[1].

After Arrival in Spain

1. **Register with Local Authorities**:

    - **Empadronamiento**: Register at your local town hall to get your certificate of registration (empadronamiento).

    - **Foreigner's Identity Number (NIE)**: Apply for your NIE, which is necessary for various administrative processes in Spain.

2. **Residency Card (TIE)**:

    - Within one month of arrival, apply for your Tarjeta de Identidad de Extranjero (TIE) at the local immigration office. This card serves as your residency permit.

Renewal and Long-Term Residency

- **First Renewal**: The initial visa is valid for one year. You can renew it for two more years, provided you continue to meet the investment and residency requirements.

- **Subsequent Renewals**: After the first renewal, you can renew the visa for another two years. After five years of continuous residency, you may apply for long-term residency.

Practical Tips

- **Visit Before Investing**: Spend some time in Spain to explore different regions and find the best location for your investment.

- **Legal Advice**: Consider hiring a local lawyer to help navigate the legal and administrative processes.

- **Tax Considerations**: Be aware of the tax implications of your investment and residency in Spain. Consult with a tax advisor to understand your obligations.

By following these steps and preparing thoroughly, you can enjoy a smooth transition to your new life in Spain.

2 HEALTHCARE

Private Health Insurance for British Retirees in Spain

Requirements for Private Health Insurance

1. **Coverage Equivalent to Spanish Public Healthcare**:
2.
    - **Comprehensive Coverage**: Your private health insurance must cover all medical services provided by the Spanish public healthcare system, including primary care, specialist consultations, hospital stays, surgeries, and emergency services.

- **No Co-Payments**: The insurance policy should not have any co-payments or deductibles. This means that all medical expenses should be covered by the insurance without requiring additional payments from you.

- **Validity**: The insurance must be valid for at least one year and renewable annually.

3. **Choosing a Provider**:

    - **Reputable Companies**: Some well-known private health insurance providers in Spain include Sanitas, Asisa, Adeslas, and DKV. These companies offer various plans tailored to the needs of expats.

    - **English-Speaking Services**: Many private health insurance providers offer services in English, which can be particularly helpful if you are not fluent in Spanish.

4. **Cost of Private Health Insurance**:

    o **Premiums**: The cost of private health insurance varies depending on your age, health condition, and the level of coverage. On average, premiums can range from €50 to €200 per month.

    o **Additional Services**: Some plans may include additional services such as dental care, optical care, and wellness programs.

Accessing Spanish Healthcare with the UK-Issued S1 Form

1. **Eligibility**:

    o **UK State Pensioners**: If you receive a UK state pension, you are eligible to use the S1 form to access Spanish healthcare services.

2.

    o **Application**: You can request the S1 form from the Overseas Healthcare Services of the NHS. You will need to provide your National Insurance number, the date you moved to Spain, and the date you will reach state retirement age.

3. **Registering the S1 Form in Spain**:

    o **INSS Registration**: Once you have the S1 form, you need to register it with the Spanish National Institute of Social Security (INSS). This can be done online or at your local INSS office.

    o **Required Documents**: You will need to provide the following documents:

        - Scanned S1 form
        - Completed application form
        - Certificate of residence (TIE) or favorable resolution from Extranjería
        - Passport
        - Census certificate (Padrón) from your local town hall
        - Proof of relationship if applying for dependents.

Benefits of Using the S1 Form:

- **Access to Public Healthcare**: Registering the S1 form entitles you to the same healthcare services as Spanish citizens, including primary care, specialist consultations, hospital treatments, and emergency services.

- **Cost Savings**: Using the S1 form can significantly reduce your healthcare costs, as you will not need to pay for private health insurance.

By ensuring you have the appropriate private health insurance or by utilizing the S1 form, you can enjoy comprehensive healthcare coverage while living in Spain.

3. FINANCIAL CONSIDERATIONS

Financial Considerations for British Retirees in Spain

Pensions

1. **Receiving Your UK State Pension in Spain:**
2.
   - **Eligibility:** You can claim your UK state pension abroad if you have paid enough UK National Insurance contributions to qualify. You must be within four months of your state pension age to make a claim.

- **How to Claim:** Contact the International Pension Centre or send the international claim form to the address provided on the form.

- **Payment Options:** Your state pension can be paid into a bank in Spain or a UK bank account. You will need the international bank account number (IBAN) and bank identification code (BIC) if you choose an overseas account. Payments can be made every four or 13 weeks.

3. **Tax Implications:**

    - **Tax Residency:** If you spend more than 183 days a year in Spain, you will be considered a tax resident and must declare your worldwide income.

    - **Double Taxation Agreement:** The UK and Spain have a double taxation agreement to prevent you from being taxed twice on the same income. Generally, your UK state pension will be taxed in Spain, not the UK.

- **Government Service Pensions:** These remain taxable only in the UK.

- **Tax Rates:** Spanish tax rates on pensions can vary, so it's advisable to consult with a tax advisor to understand your specific obligations.

4. **Private Pensions:**

    - **QROPS:** You can transfer your UK private pension to a Qualifying Recognised Overseas Pension Scheme (QROPS) in Spain. This can offer tax advantages but requires careful consideration and possibly permission from HMRC.

    - **Tax-Free Lump Sum:** Spain does not recognize the UK's tax-free lump sum. If you wish to take a lump sum, it's best to do so while still a UK resident to avoid Spanish taxes.

Cost of Living

1. **Regional Variations:**

    o **Coastal Areas and Major Cities:** Places like Barcelona, Madrid, and the Costa del Sol are known for their higher cost of living. These areas offer vibrant cultural scenes, excellent amenities, and a large expat community, but at a premium price.

    o **Affordable Regions:** Andalusia (e.g., Seville, Granada), Extremadura (e.g., Badajoz), and Murcia (e.g., Cartagena) are more budget-friendly options. These regions offer a lower cost of living while still providing a high quality of life.

2. **Housing Costs:**

    o **Renting vs. Buying:** Renting can be more flexible and less expensive upfront, while buying property can be a good long-term investment. Coastal areas and major cities tend to have higher property prices compared to rural areas.

- **Average Costs:** In more affordable regions, you can expect to pay around €500-€800 per month for a one-bedroom apartment, while in more expensive areas, this can rise to €1,000-€1,500.

3. **Daily Expenses:**

    - **Groceries and Dining:** The cost of groceries and dining out is generally lower than in the UK. Local markets and supermarkets offer fresh produce at reasonable prices, and dining out can be quite affordable, especially in smaller towns.

    - **Utilities and Transportation:** Utilities (electricity, heating, cooling, water, garbage) for a standard apartment can cost around €100-€150 per month. Public transportation is efficient and affordable, with monthly passes costing around €40-€60.

By understanding these financial

considerations, you can better plan for a comfortable and enjoyable retirement in Spain.

4 HOUSING

Housing: Renting vs. Buying in Spain

Renting

Advantages:

1. Flexibility:

- **Mobility:** Renting allows you to move easily if you decide to explore different regions of Spain or if your circumstances change.

- Short-Term Commitment: You can rent on a short-term basis, such as holiday rentals or medium-term rentals, which are popular on Spain's Costas.

2. **Lower Upfront Costs:**

       o **Initial Expenses:** Renting requires a security deposit and the first month's rent, which is significantly lower than the down payment and other costs associated with buying.

       o **No Maintenance Costs:** The landlord is responsible for maintaining the property, including repairs and replacements of essential items like heating, air conditioning, and water heaters.

3. **Reduced Financial Risk:**

       o **Market Fluctuations:** Renting shields you from the risks associated with property market fluctuations. You won't be affected by changes in property values.

       o **Disadvantages:** Temporary Tenure: Rental contracts typically last for five years, after which they can be renewed or terminated with the landlord's agreement.

       o

2. **Lack of Stability:**

    o **Potential Rent Increases:** New rental laws in Spain cap rent increases, but new contracts may still be subject to higher rents due to supply and demand.

3. **No Equity Building:**

    o No Investment Return: Renting does not allow you to build equity or benefit from property appreciation.

Buying

Advantages:

1. **Long-Term Investment:**

    o **Equity Building:** Buying a property allows you to build equity over time. Property values in Spain have shown steady growth, making it an attractive long-term investment.
    o Potential Appreciation: Historically, the Spanish property market has experienced growth, offering

potential returns on your investment.

2. **Customization and Stability:**

    o **Personalization**: Homeownership allows you to customize and renovate your property to suit your preferences.

    o **Permanent Residence:** Owning a home provides stability and a sense of permanence, which can be particularly appealing for retirees.

3. **Tax Benefits:**

    o **Deductions:** Homeowners may be eligible for certain tax deductions related to mortgage interest and property taxes.

Disadvantages:

1. **Higher Upfront Costs:**

    o **Initial Investment**: Buying a property involves substantial upfront costs, including a down payment (usually 20-30% of the property price), taxes, notary fees, and potential mortgage costs.

2.
- o **Ongoing Expenses:** Homeowners are responsible for maintenance, repairs, property taxes, and community fees.

3. **Reduced Flexibility:**

    - o **Commitment**: Buying ties you to a specific location, making it more challenging to move if your circumstances change.

    - o **Selling Challenges:** Selling a property can take time, and market conditions may affect the sale price.

4. **Legal and Administrative Requirements:**

    - o **NIE Number:** Non-residents must obtain a Foreigner Identity Number (NIE) to complete any financial transactions, including property purchases[3].
    - o Legal Advice: It's advisable to hire a local lawyer to navigate the legal and administrative processes involved in buying property in

Spain[3].

Conclusion

Deciding whether to rent or buy in Spain depends on your personal circumstances, financial situation, and long-term plans. Renting offers flexibility and lower upfront costs, making it ideal for those who are not yet familiar with the area or prefer mobility. Buying, on the other hand, provides long-term investment potential, stability, and the opportunity to build equity. Carefully weigh the pros and cons of each option to make an informed decision that best suits your needs.

5 CULTURAL AND SOCIAL SUGGESTIONS

Retiring to Spain can be a wonderful experience, especially if you embrace the local culture and social interactions. Here are some key aspects to consider:

1. Language

- **Learning Spanish**: While many Spaniards, especially in tourist areas, speak English, learning Spanish will greatly enhance your experience. It shows respect for the local culture and helps in daily interactions.

- **Language Classes**: Consider enrolling in language classes. Many communities offer courses specifically for expatriates.

2. Social Etiquette

- **Greetings**: Spaniards typically greet each other with a kiss on both cheeks, even when meeting for the first time. A handshake is also common in more formal settings.

- **Personal Space**: Spaniards tend to stand closer to each other when talking compared to British norms. This is a sign of friendliness, not intrusion.

3. Community Engagement

- **Local Events**: Participate in local festivals and events. Spain has a rich calendar of fiestas, from local town celebrations to national holidays.

- **Volunteer Work**: Engaging in volunteer work can be a great way to meet people and integrate into the community.

4. Daily Life

- **Café Culture**: Spain has a vibrant café culture. Spending time in local cafés, enjoying a coffee or a meal, is a common social activity.

- **Meal Times**: Spaniards eat later than Brits. Lunch is usually around 2-3 PM, and dinner can be as late as 9-10 PM. Adjusting to these times can help you fit in better.

5. Activities and Hobbies

- **Clubs and Groups**: Join local clubs or groups that match your interests, such as hiking, cooking, or book clubs. This is a great way to meet like-minded people.

- **Sports**: Football is hugely popular in Spain. Attending local matches or joining a sports club can be a good way to socialize.

6. Healthcare and Services

- **Healthcare System**: Spain has an excellent healthcare system. Registering with a local doctor and understanding how the system works will be beneficial.

- **Services for Expats**: Many areas with large expat communities offer services and support groups specifically for foreigners.

7. Financial and Legal Considerations

- **Banking**: Opening a local bank account can simplify financial transactions.

- **Legal Advice**: Consulting with a local lawyer can help you navigate any legal requirements, especially regarding property and residency.

8. Overcoming Challenges

- **Cultural Differences**: Be patient and open-minded about cultural differences. What might seem unusual at first can become a cherished part of your new life.

- **Building Relationships**: Building meaningful relationships takes time. Be proactive in reaching out and making connections.

9. Integration Tips

- **Respect Local Customs**: Showing respect for local customs and traditions will help you gain acceptance.

- **Stay Informed**: Keep up with local news and events to stay connected with your community.

By embracing these cultural and social aspects, you can enjoy a fulfilling and enriching retirement in Spain.

6 TAXATION

Retiring to Spain as a British citizen involves understanding various tax implications. Here's a detailed overview:

1. Tax Residency

- **Residency Status**: If you spend more than 183 days in Spain in a calendar year, you are considered a tax resident. As a tax resident, you are liable to pay taxes on your worldwide income in Spain.

2. Income Tax

- **Pensions**: Pensions are generally taxed as income in Spain. The tax rates are progressive, ranging from 19% to 47% depending on the amount.

  - **State Pensions**: Treated as earned income and taxed at standard rates.

  - **Private Pensions**: Also taxed as income.

  - **Government Pensions**: If you receive a government pension from the UK, it may be exempt from Spanish tax but still considered for calculating your overall tax rate.

3. Double Taxation Treaty

- **Avoiding Double Taxation**: The UK and Spain have a double taxation treaty to prevent you from being taxed twice on the same income. This treaty ensures that you can offset taxes paid in one country against taxes due in the other.

4. Wealth Tax

- **Wealth Tax**: Spain imposes a wealth tax on assets exceeding €700,000. The rates vary by region and can range from 0.2% to 2.5%.

5. Capital Gains Tax

- **Property Sales**: If you sell property in the UK or Spain, you may be liable for capital gains tax. The rates in Spain range from 19% to 23%.

6. Inheritance and Gift Tax

- **Inheritance Tax**: Spain has inheritance tax, but the rates and exemptions vary by region. For example, in Andalucia, direct family members can inherit up to €1,000,000 tax-free.

- **Forced Heirship**: Spanish law requires that two-thirds of an estate must go to children which can be overridden by using the European Succession Regulation (Brussels IV) to apply UK inheritance laws.

7. Tax Allowances

- **Personal Allowance**: The personal allowance in Spain is €5,550, increasing to €6,700 for those over 65 and €8,100 for those over 75.

8. Practical Steps

- **Registering as a Resident**: Ensure you register as a resident if you plan to stay more than six months a year.

- **Tax Returns**: File annual tax returns in Spain, detailing your worldwide income.

9. Professional Advice

- **Consult a Tax Advisor**: Given the complexity of international tax laws, it's advisable to consult a tax advisor who specializes in expatriate taxation to ensure compliance and optimize your tax situation.

Understanding these tax implications can help you plan better for your retirement in Spain.

7 LEGAL AND ADMINISTRATIVE

Retiring to Spain as a British citizen involves navigating several legal and administrative matters, especially post-Brexit. Here's a detailed guide to help you understand the key aspects:

1. Residency Permits

- **Non-Lucrative Visa**: This is a popular option for retirees. It allows you to live in Spain without working. You need to demonstrate sufficient financial means and have private health insurance.

- **Golden Visa:** If you invest at least €500,000 in Spanish real estate, you can apply for this visa. It offers residency for you and your family.

- **Application Process:** Apply at the Spanish consulate in the UK. You'll need documents like your passport, proof of income, health insurance, and a clean criminal record.

2. Healthcare

- **Private Health Insurance:** Required for the non-lucrative visa. Ensure it covers all medical expenses without co-payments.

- **Public Healthcare:** Once you become a resident, you may be eligible for public healthcare. Register at your local health center with your residency card.

3. Financial Requirements

- Proof of Income: For the non-lucrative visa, you need to show a stable income or savings. The minimum required is around €27,115 per year for the main applicant, plus additional amounts for dependents[1].
- Bank Account: Opening a local bank account can simplify financial transactions and bill payments.

3. Property Purchase

- **Legal Advice:** Hire a local lawyer to help with property transactions. They can ensure the property has no debts or legal issues.

- **NIE Number:** You'll need a Número de Identificación de Extranjero (NIE) for any financial transactions, including buying property.

4. Taxes

- **Income Tax**: As a resident, you'll pay taxes on your worldwide income. Spain has a progressive tax system with rates ranging from 19% to 47%.

- Wealth Tax: Applicable on assets exceeding €700,000, with rates varying by region.

- Double Taxation Treaty: The UK and Spain have a treaty to avoid double taxation. This means you won't be taxed twice on the same income.

5. Legal Documentation

- **Residency Card:** Once your visa is approved, you'll need to apply for a Tarjeta de Identidad de Extranjero (TIE) within 30 days of arrival[1].
- **Registration:** Register with the local town hall (empadronamiento) to access local services and benefits.

6. Driving License

- **Exchange Your License:** You can exchange your UK driving license for a Spanish one. This process involves a medical check and some paperwork.

7. Social Integration

- **Language**: Learning Spanish will help you integrate better and navigate daily life more easily.

- **Community Involvement:** Engage in local activities and events to build a social network and feel more at home.

8. Professional Assistance

- **Legal and Financial Advisors:** Consider hiring professionals who specialize in expatriate services to help you with the transition and ensure compliance with all legal requirements.

By understanding and preparing for these legal and administrative matters, you can enjoy a smooth transition to your new life in Spain.

CHAPTER 8. PRACTICAL STEPS

Retiring to Spain as a British citizen involves several practical steps to ensure a smooth transition. Here's a detailed guide to help you through the process:

1. Research and planning

- **Location**: Choose the right location based on your preferences. Popular areas include costa del sol, costa Blanca, and the Balearic islands.

- **Visit first**: Spend some time in your chosen area before making a final decision. This will help you understand the local lifestyle and amenities.

2. Visa and residency

- **Non-lucrative visa**: apply for this visa if you plan to retire without working. You need to show sufficient financial means and have private health insurance.

- **Golden visa**: if you invest at least €500,000 in Spanish real estate, you can apply for this visa.

- **Application process**: submit your visa application at the Spanish consulate in the UK. Required documents include your passport, proof of income, health insurance, and a clean criminal record.

3. Financial preparation

- **Proof of income**: for the non-lucrative visa, you need to demonstrate a stable income or savings. The minimum required is around €27,115 per year for the main applicant.

- **Bank account**: open a local bank account

to manage your finances and pay bills more easily.

4. Healthcare

- **Private health insurance**: required for the non-lucrative visa. Ensure it covers all medical expenses without co-payments.

- **Public healthcare**: once you become a resident, you may be eligible for public healthcare. Register at your local health center with your residency card.

5. Property purchase or rental

- **Legal advice**: hire a local lawyer to assist with property transactions. They can ensure the property has no debts or legal issues.

- **Nie number**: obtain a número de identificación de extranjero (nie) for any financial transactions, including buying property.

6. Taxes

- **Income tax**: as a resident, you'll pay taxes on your worldwide income. Spain has a progressive tax system with rates ranging from 19% to 47%.

- **Wealth tax**: applicable on assets exceeding €700,000, with rates varying by region.

- **Double taxation treaty**: the uk and spain have a treaty to avoid double taxation. This means you won't be taxed twice on the same income.

7. Legal documentation

- **Residency card**: once your visa is approved, apply for a tarjeta de identidad de extranjero (tie) within 30 days of arrival.

- **Registration**: register with the local town hall (empadronamiento) to access local services and benefits.

8. Driving license

- **Exchange your license**: you can exchange your UK driving license for a Spanish one. This process involves a medical check and some paperwork.

9. Social integration

- **Language**: learning Spanish will help you integrate better and navigate daily life more easily.

- **Community involvement**: engage in local activities and events to build a social network and feel more at home.

10. Professional assistance

- **Legal and financial advisors**: consider hiring professionals who specialize in expatriate services to help you with the transition and ensure compliance with all legal requirements.

By following these practical steps, you can enjoy a smooth transition to your new life in Spain.

ABOUT THE AUTHOR

Arthur Crandon is a retired lawyer and a prolific writer. He is British and grew up in a rural community in Somerset. He has lived in England, Wales, Hong Kong and the Philippines and now spends most of his time in the Philippines with his Visayan wife and their son.

He loves to hear from anyone who has anything to do with the Philippines – you can email him anytime on:

ac@arthurcrandon.co.uk

Made in the USA
Las Vegas, NV
31 March 2025